Horror Story Asia
Battling an Asian Giant

JIM KAYALAR, DBA (ABD)

ISBN: 1508641307
ISBN-13: 978-1508641308

DEDICATION

To YEK.

CONTENTS

ACKNOWLEDGMENTS

FOREWORD

You will see their fancy advertisements on TV and in glamorous magazines. You will see their corporate sponsorship logos at sporting events. They look sophisticated and established. Yet the law means nothing to these organizations. They will adhere to the minimum standards of the law wherever they operate. In countries and markets where there is no rule of law they will leave all pretence of civility behind and lie, steal and connive to achieve their goals at your expense. Yet their owners will be fawned upon by the media and they will have superstar status wherever they go. This is a small attempt to lift the veil just a little bit to take a look at what these 800 pound gorillas are really about.

Thank you for purchasing "Horror Story Asia - Hatay Pacific Airlines". This is a fictionalized true story. Hatay Pacific Airlines, part of the Qwire Group domiciled in England have caused damage to my health and my finances. They have stolen a year of my life. Unfortunately after trying all venues there is nothing more I can do. I am just one individual with limited means fighting against a well oiled, well funded multinational giant that is playing dirty.

After working for nearly 30 years in different parts of the world I have come across many unethical organizations and managers. You come across all kinds of swindlers the more you live, the more you work and the more you experience. I have seen my part of the bad and ugly but most of them don't come close to the bad and ugly at Hatay Pacific Airlines. This is their story.

1: HATAY PACIFIC 800 POUND GORILLA

This horror story is about Hatay Pacific Airlines owned jointly between the world renown Qwire Group and a Chinese Airline. Many of you may think that Hatay Pacific is a Chinese company. Well, they are not. They are owned by a privately held English Corporation that goes by the name of Qwire Group and operates out of the City of Westminster, England. They just pretend to be Asian and Chinese because they can then operate outside the legal and ethical restrictions their country of origin poses.

Before I go on, let me state that I have travelled to Hong Kong at least 15-20 times, starting in the mid 90's and really love the place. Hatay Pacific tried to make me out as anti-Hong Kong and anti-China. I am not. I have also travelled extensively in China and respect the Chinese civilization and all its contributions to humanity. My wife and I continue to travel to Hong Kong despite her bad memories being robbed at knife point by a gang of five men in Hong Kong's Wan Shai district, an upscale shopping district in Hong Kong.

"This was supposed to have been their great annual family vacation" Jim McKay thought. They had lived and worked in numerous countries in Asia, she a banker and he a management consultant/academic. Once a year they took a long three week break from the tropical Asian heat and travelled to the colder Northern Hemisphere. It wasn't always back home to New Jersey but it was more often than not. They had strenuously planned their three week holiday to New York City and Canada, bought the plane tickets with Hatay Pacific Airlines from Hong Kong to New York JFK airport and Air Canada, booked the hotels in NYC, London (Ontario-Canada), Montreal and Quebec. This vacation had been planned in detail and was supposed to have been the highlight of the year.

Unfortunately the imbeciles at Hatay Pacific had messed it up for them. McKay in all his years as a business executive, management consultant and academic had never come across a company that was so badly managed and so good at mistreating its customers. Add shameless, not to mention conniving and threatening. One could add many other impolite and profound phrases to describe this organization. Unethical, criminal, dumb etc.

I had used all that and much worse when corresponding with Hatay Pacific and when I had drawn them through their own bull crap. Several times in fact. 800 pound Gorillas usually are a lot of crap! There was a lot of crap about Hatay Pacific on the internet after all. There was Hatay Pacific getting caught in a major price fixing scandal. There was the Hatay Pacific sex scandals in the cockpit, with the cockpit and anywhere and everywhere between company management and crew and between the crew and everyone else. Everything was on the internet and one needed only to Google "Hatay Pacific Scandal" or "Hatay Pacific Sex Scandal". The instigators recorded everything on the cell phones and somehow it leaked! There are also numerous blogs and websites that detail how Hatay Pacific mistreated paying customers. Apparently they have been doing this for quite some time now and have been getting away with it.

There's plenty of triple "X" rated Hatay Pacific porn, slutty pictures of Hatay Pacific air crew in their red uniforms exposing themselves on the plane and of course the same red uniforms performing oral sex on a Hatay Pacific Captain on the internet. The only thing that was not clear was whether the oral sex was before, during or after the flight or before, during and after!

Anyways, just in case some of you reading this didn't understand the term "oral", I looked the term up on the Google and found some other slang terms " Lewinskiying it, earn red wings, auto fellatio". I am not bullshitting you. Look for yourself. I especially liked the "earn red wings" one. Since the Hatay Pacific outfit is already red, and they already have the wings too, ditto! I think a new slang term in addition to the infamous "mile high club" should be "Baby, Hatay Airlines me"! (For those of you who know me in person I can already see you thinking "We used to know McKay as a polite and kind person. Have we misjudged him or what has gotten into him?" Well, I am mad and I know you can tell by the type of language I am using).

I am not enjoying writing this and some of you who might actually know me or have read my previous publications might be thinking why on earth I am doing this given my professional experience of over 30 years in international business, my academic credentials and international publications (recently published in Chinese as well). I am a serious, professional and courteous person, respectful of all cultures, religions and peoples that I have worked with in 28 countries.

I am sharing this "Horror Story" to name and shame an unscrupulous business organization that has damaged my health, usurped a year of my life, broken the law, threatened me and messed up a vacation. I am doing this because I am but just one righteous individual fighting against a giant organization for over two years to get what is rightfully mine. I am doing this despite all that Hatay Pacific has ditched out so far to damage and discredit me. I have not flinched, not given up an inch of my determination and continue to seek justice.

I have named and shamed them, I have reported and continue to report what I believe to be their criminal conduct to governmental and non governmental agencies. Many of these organizations have shunned their obligation. Unfortunately they are too scared of Hatay Pacific and the repercussions.

My activism has changed the way Hatay Pacific operates. As a result of my activities they have had to change the way they do business, change their social media strategy and have had to start censorship of their content as a result. They have had to spend hundreds of hours to try and "make me go away" and wear me out. They have used all kinds of resources and people in their network to attack and discredit me. It's called character assassination. It hasn't worked I have dealt with each attack and outwitted and outsmarted each and every one as you will soon see.

"Hatay Pacific, I am still here, standing straight and proud. Look at how you have had to change the way you do business and the hundreds of hours you have spent trying to cover your butt and fight me. Just like I said you would".

I use each opportunity I get every single day, whether in my classroom, online presence or through word of mouth with friends, relatives and peers to impress upon people, (Read potential customers) not to fly Hatay Pacific. Here is another opportunity! "Do not fly Hatay Pacific".

In direct lost sales dollar value (Not counting my family's yearly business) Hatay Pacific have already lost several times the dollar amount of what they would have paid to fairly compensate me for my loss. I have had several large organizations cancel their Hatay Pacific bookings and instead purchase tickets with their competitors. Double Whammy! Hatay Pacific not only lost sales but I have helped their competitors get additional business and make more money as a result. Hatay Pacific has lost and will continue to lose.

The altercation with Hatay Pacific at the moment of this writing is now into its third year. They thought they could "screw me over" and get away with it because of their size, expensive lawyers, network of employees and affiliates.

Why this altercation and confrontation?

Simple, Hatay Pacific stole a year of my life and did not own up to their mistake.

2: A LITTLE BIT ABOUT LIFE IN ASIA

My wife Jasmine travels mostly in Asia and has a 50 percent travel load. The pre-business trip planning and errands and then the post-business trip reporting takes up so much of her time that we are constantly trying to scrape quality time together. My business trips are not as frequent but usually last longer; anywhere between a month to six months.

It's hard to maintain a long distance marriage despite Skype, email, SMS messages and cell phones and what have you. The holidays usually help us get back together and put things into perspective. Many couples today face the same challenges. When living in Asia there are all kinds of additional challenges and when travelling for business or pleasure you learn not to take anything for granted. Anything could happen anytime. We have had our share of failed coup attempts, natural disasters, earthquakes, typhoons and countless floods. As a rule of thumb, when living in Asia you learn to keep your expectations low and to be pleasantly surprised when that airport pickup is on time, you were actually given the type of room you had reserved, the front desk didn't try to inflate your bill and all that was advertised on the website was actually there.

I am not only talking about Asian brands. Even global brands in Asia do not manage or probably even attempt to upkeep global standards of service and hygiene despite charging global prices. This is probably what is the most unfair. You end up paying top Manhattan prices (I am choosing Manhattan because of the exorbitant prices even three star midtown hotels charge for a basic room) for a product or service that is far inferior in quality, in a developing country that only boasts a fifth of the comparable annual income per person.

To put it simply, during our tenure in Asia we have had basically seen a whole lot of variations on misrepresentation, bending the facts, outright lying, not offering promised services and of course the sale of inferior products/services. Once there is a service delivery failure, (Regardless of type of company) be it a hotel, car rental or airline company, you either have to intervene immediately and demand the service, get compensation or forget about it. For the most part there is no service delivery failure recovery effort. To be fair, there are the likes of Singapore Airlines that adhere to higher standards and do try to rectify service delivery failures. In our Asia experience promises made even by really large organizations as advertised on CNN, BBC and Time etc. to correct a service delivery failure and offer compensation at a future date are never kept and even if you persist they eventually wear you down.

Attempts to use the local legal system as a foreigner in an Asian setting are futile as you have basically no chance to either pursue the matter or have too little time to understand and work the system and overcome communication barriers. Many expatriates living in Asia agree that most of the time "they took you" and the only thing you could do was to move on. "Suck it up, you have been had once again".

3: MY BIG LOSS

I had brought along my doctoral dissertation proposal on "Competitive Strategies of Asian Firms" to work on during the 16 hour long flight with Hatay Pacific Airlines from Hong Kong to New York. I like to work in soft copy format and then transfer my writings to my computer. I have numerous health issues of which diabetes is the biggest challenge to manage on a long haul flight. I had taken onboard an assortment of low glycemic foods and glucose lowering medication as well as my blood test kit to measure my sugar levels in case things got out of hand. We had requested a plastic bag to keep all our little items together and a flight attendant had kindly provided us with a white Hatay Pacific plastic bag. Jasmine had also placed some of her own medications, cosmetics and food items into the bag.

The flight was largely uneventful and we had travelled as comfortably as was possible in Economy class by spending an extra $200 per person to get bulkhead seats that provided more legroom on the 16 hour flight. The seats on the aged Boeing plane provided little lumbar support and were uncomfortable. The food was nothing special, the portions were kind of small, (They seem to be getting smaller every year) we were served only two meals throughout the trip and had to rely on snacks to fill up.

Jasmine had once again stuffed all our little bits and pieces into the white Hatay Pacific plastic bag, including my dissertation notebook, USB stick, pens and pencils and placed it under our seat. A flight attendant had insisted that the bag be taken out from under the seat, tied up tightly and stowed in an overhead compartment. Unfortunately the overhead compartments were full and the stewardesses had stored the bag in the galley and had returned it upon landing. We had put the bag inside our carry-on luggage and disembarked. I remember how everyone including the crew were happy to finally get out of the plane after 16 hours.

JFK airport was a little rowdy but efficient, the cold weather was invigorating and we were checked in at our midtown Manhattan hotel an hour after disembarking from the plane. I had felt my blood sugar levels drop uncomfortably low and had taken out the white Hatay Pacific bag to get a diabetic protein bar, alas instead to find a bag of thrash. The flight attendant had mistakenly mixed up the bags in her haste and had given us a bag of thrash instead.

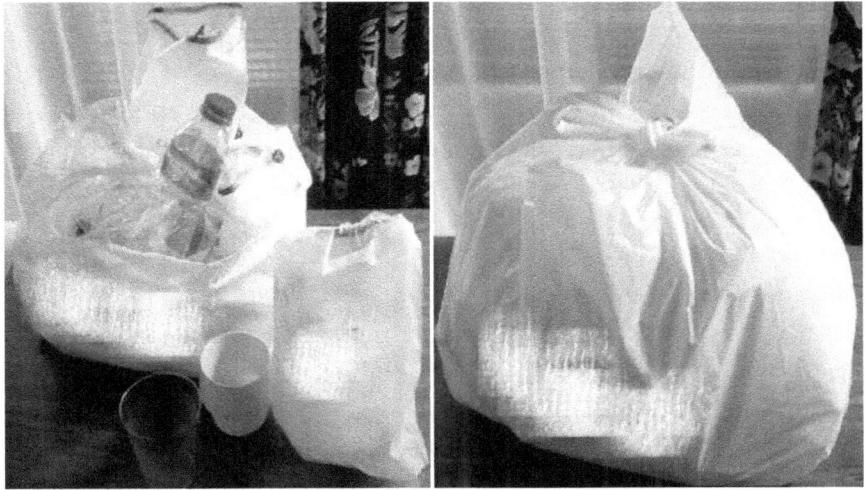

Thrash Bag Picture One   Thrash Bag Picture Two

4: INITIAL DEALINGS

Fortunately we had with us a tablet computer and were able to access the internet from the hotel lobby and had immediately called the numbers on the Hatay Pacific USA web site. I should say "tried". The given 1-800 number was constantly busy and inaccessible. Next we tried the other two local numbers we got from their website. Of the two numbers we called, the voicemail of one of the numbers was full and thus unoperational. After numerous attempts we were finally able to get through to the other number and leave a voicemail.

We also tried to send emails with the heading "Urgent" to the contact email addresses provided by the Hatay Pacific global web site. One of the emails bounced back as unoperational. If Hatay Pacific was making sure that nobody contacted them, they were doing a damn good job.

Two hours after our initial attempts to contact Hatay Pacific we got a call back from a Hatay Pacific employee, a Mr. Marc Womack. We once again recited what had happened and he basically told us that it was probably too late to do anything about our lost bag and in any case it was beyond his pay grade to do anything about it. His parting comments were full of doom and gloom as our bag was probably already in a landfill (That's were apparently all bags from the galley go) and suggested that we call the same number that we had called earlier and ask for a supervisor call back. I couldn't help but think "why do organizations even bother to construct organizational charts and fill boxes and then not give authority to people in charge?".

Marc Womack had responded to the voice mail, done his job and passed on responsibility and accountability to another employee. We were going to see more of this behavior at Hatay Pacific. At this early stage of the service delivery failure any action or initiative on the part of Hatay Pacific could have recovered our bag. Authority without responsibility. Authority without accountability. Play the process, push decisions upstairs and move on. I am thinking back to 9.11. This is exactly the same line of thinking that augmented the effort of the terrorists when they took down the World Trade Center and hit the Pentagon.

Why do you think Marc Womack did not bother call his supervisor himself? Maybe he could care less and didn't want any extra work on a Saturday, maybe it was a political play to make the supervisor look bad and irresponsive, etc. In any case nothing happened. All they had needed to do was to make a couple of phone calls to locate the three or four garbage bags coming out of the plane galleys and spend three to five minutes to find our bag. In legal terms this is called willful negligence.

I can see you go: So what's the big fuss about the bag. What was in the bag?

Firstly, a large part of my diabetic medicines good for the three week trip. I usually have these in my cabin bag just in case my checked in baggage gets lost. As a result of their loss I had to ration them and take lower doses. Travelling to and from Canada and back to the USA there was no time to get certified as a diabetic which entailed going to a *endocrinologist (Diabetes* doctor), get all kinds of expensive blood test, return back to the doctor to get certified as a diabetic, go to a pharmacy and have prescriptions filled out and lastly pick them up. Add to that the extra cost which would have run into several thousand dollars. Having to adjust my medical regimen negatively affected my health as I was having glucose spikes.

Secondly, my doctoral dissertation proposal. Anybody who has attempted or completed a doctoral dissertation proposal knows how much hard work goes into it. All the countless hours of research, writing, rewriting followed by yet more research and sleepless nights. It had taken me close to six months to develop.

Thirdly, a USB stick containing my numerous publications in different stages of development. Another six months worth of work product. Furthermore numerous corporate agreements and confidential contracts which automatically exposed me and Hatay Pacific to third party liability.

Fourthly, Jasmine's prescription medicines, cosmetics and food items.

Fifthly, my favorite pen and mechanical pencil. Don't laugh at this because as writers we all have our favorite pens and pencils that help ward of writers block. It's a psychological thing...

The Hatay Pacific Horror Story Unfolds

The supervisor callback from Hatay Pacific came two days later. Mr. Haydn Wagner a soft spoken Hatay Pacific employee assured us that they would do everything to recover our bag. Two days later! The plane apparently was still parked on the tarmac at JFK. A late post hoc effort was apparently undertaken to find our bag according to Mr. Wagner, something which might or might not be true. Thinking back this was probably a lie as Hatay Pacific lied to us so many times.

Wagner's take was that thrash from the plane was first recycled in their kitchen and then thrown away. Unfortunately after checking with ground crews we were informed that our bag had not been recovered during recycling. That was odd given that the bags content was not thrash.

Losing all hope of recovering our possessions and seeing that Hatay Pacific was trying hard to cover up the matter, I asked for Mr. Wagner's email address and subsequently sent him an email detailing our losses. The email bounced back because the email given by Wagner was wrong. Wagner had given us a wrong email address! Maybe the poor sod didn't know his email address!

I tried numerous times to contact Hatay Pacific:

1. Email to their frequent flyer assistance desk in Hong Kong. No reply.

2. Email to their lost baggage contact email at JFK. Email bounced back. Unoperational.

3. Email to their North America service desk at JFK. No reply.

4. Email to Haydn Wagner – Gave me wrong email. Unoperational.

I was desperate to establish that the bag had been lost by Hatay Pacific and to protect myself against third party liability due to the contents of the USB stick and kept calling and emailing Hatay Pacific and leaving voicemails, all the while trying to run errands and enjoy our "vacation" in New York.

After several days of trying I was finally able get a hold of Wagner who shifted accountability and responsibility to yet another Hatay Pacific employee, a Mrs. Lana Ravioli of the Hatay Pacific New York office who handled lost bag claims. I did however start to wonder why Wagner couldn't just have written an email to this person himself. At that stage I hadn't realized the extent of the run around, lying and cheating on the side of Hatay Pacific on top of the bull crap I was going to witness.

Turns out, the conduct of the junior Hatay Pacific employee Mrs. Lana Ravioli who was in charge of filing lost bag claims was exemplary of the ethical and legal business integrity of an organization that will lie, cheat and threaten to abuse its customers. Ravioli was nowhere to be found for the next three days.

We called all the Hatay Pacific phone numbers we could find and lo and behold this time phones that were actually working, but just like her boss Ravioli was either out of the office or not returning calls. The Qwire group would be proud I am sure.

In the business of customer care we call this the delaying of communication and interaction with the customer, wasting their time, making the process difficult, extorting a high level of effort and finally cooling them off and making them go away. There are statistics as to how many unsatisfied customers will actually report or complain when a service delivery failure happen. Statistics indicate that most customers will give up after a couple of failed attempts or when it becomes too hard to and time consuming to deal with the matter.

After three days of pursuing her day and night, Ravioli called us at our hotel and left us a voice mail at 11.58 a.m. informing us that she had tried to contact us "so many times" and for us to call her until 12 noon. A full two minutes of access or she would be gone! Dear Ravioli, most phones in North America have time stamp functions. You need to polish up your bull crap!

Thank you Hatay Pacific for not only losing the bag but giving us, the already anguished customers a full two minute lead time to respond! After another three days of this farce we finally called Ravioli at 5.30 a.m. in the morning right after her shift started, and this is on our so called holiday!

Hatay Pacific employee Mrs. Ravioli was very confrontational, accusative and outright rude. I am sure she was very unhappy to be finally talking to customers she had so far successfully eluded. A shouting match ensued at 5.30 a.m. and I could hear her boss Wagner next to her giving her encouragement and guidance. Let me express my frustration and anger at these two despicable people by leaving an empty space, an empty space that you can fill for me. Nothing personal, all business! You ..... , ..., ...

My wife who is more sensitive when it comes to dealing with the likes of Wagner, Ravioli and Hatay Pacific was extremely upset. I wanted her to have the best holiday under the circumstances, but seeing me suffer and the toll it took to confront Hatay Pacific made her even more upset. She cried a lot during the trip and afterwards.

From my many years of working in Asia I know that shouting and rudeness is a form of negotiation tactic which is commonly used especially against foreigners with the aim of intimidating your opponent. Well you guessed it. It didn't work. I wonder if Hatay Pacific in the USA or Europe especially trains its employees to be rude? It's clear that they are all trained not to provide customer care and avoid any kind of compensation and restitution but can't you at least pretend that your people can respond to angry Western customers in the

Western way with a degree of respect and caring. The Qwire group should be proud!

A new twist to what could have happened to our bag was supplied by Ravioli: "Hatay Pacific incinerates all garbage that comes out of its planes" rather than their previous statements to the fact that they were disposing waste in landfills or recycling. "So what is it Hatay Pacific, landfill, recycling or incineration? Or just more lies to cover your butt's?"

Five days after Hatay Pacific lost our bag we finally got an email response from Ravioli at the Hatay Pacific New York office. The email carried the heading "Without Prejudice". Wow! "Without Prejudice" is a legal term which basically states " We accept no responsibility and you may not use this correspondence in court". Another great attempt by Hatay Pacific to cover its butt.

In their email Hatay Pacific asked for a list of lost articles which I was happy to provide. This meant taking time off from our "vacation", finding a PC and writing to them again. Their next move was to ask for receipts to prove that those articles were actually in the bag. I usually don't carry receipts of items with me and I don't know anybody that does. Hatay Pacific was again trying to make things as hard as possible.

The contents of the Hatay thrash bag that we were given had started to smell and I was forced to take pictures of the bag and throw it away. Naturally no attempt was made by Hatay Pacific to visually inspect the bag of thrash and ascertain its existence. I had dealt with similar unethical organizations in the past who had accused me of trying to defraud them after similar service delivery failures. A photograph usually silenced them. In fact this was the direction that Hatay Pacific was trying to take when I supplied them with a photo of the thrash bag.

Going back to Hatay Pacific making things as difficult as possible for the customer play. Some of the items in the bag were purchased in Europe others in Asia and some in the USA. Even if I had purchased or repurchased everything in New York, travelling to purchase a certain prescription cream for my wife only sold in Queens would have taken at least half a day and cost me upward of $100 for transport. You think that Hatay Pacific will cover the lost time and cost of transport?

I could have of course gone to the nearest store and purchased something similar and submitted the invoice to Hatay Pacific, but for one I didn't do that because I am honest and for two Hatay Pacific stated that they "may consider" my claim and would probably resort to all kinds of new shenanigans not to pay. Thirdly, they absolutely refused to even "consider" the value of the dissertation proposal, and the first and third party liability as a result of the confidential contents on the USB stick.

Fortunately at the time of this writing I have not received any emails trying to extort money out of me nor have my semi-finished publications been published or flaunted online. In good will I absolved Hatay Pacific of the third party liability they had incurred as result of losing my bag and informed them thus.

As I predicted Hatay Pacific in ensuing emails challenged me to prove that the items I claimed were indeed in the bag and accused me of fraud, despite the pictures I had supplied them. I was naive to think "Who would knowingly concoct a plan to steal a bag of thrash from Hatay Pacific and then pretend it contained all kinds of items of value and ask for compensation". All my efforts did not make a difference. Several weeks went by without any headway. I then contacted the Hatay Pacific Chief Executive Officer, Chief Operating Officer and anybody else I could find.

5: MASTER'S OF DECEPTION AND CUSTOMER UNCARE

Within days I received an email from their Customer Service manager in Hong Kong, a Ms. Lizzy Lee.

Customer service manager Ms. Lee seemed very professional and smooth. I even started to think that this was an isolated incident and that maybe the Hatay Pacific customer relations office would be different. In her email Lee stated that she would look into the matter and report back. Two weeks after her initial email there was still no update so I once again contacted her.

In our MBA business courses and executive training sessions we always teach that a quick, direct and responsive communication followed by a timely service delivery failure recovery will help make the customer happy and retain their business. The opposite is true if you want to lose a customer.

Another concept we teach is the customer lifetime value. Let's say I travel between Hong Kong and New York once every year. If I am 50 now and will travel till I am 65, that comes to 15 flights over the remainder of my lifetime value as a customer. So if I am unhappy with a company, the company not only loses my lifetime value of 15 flights but I also take my money to a competitor. If every year I spend $3,000 on a plane ticket between Hong Kong and New York, the company has lost $45,000 in revenue and their competitors have just made $45,000. More on this later. Back to Hatay Pacific Hong Kong customer relations manager Mrs. Lee.

Ms. Lee wrote back several days later informing me that they apparently had been busy contacting the crew of the flight which had lost our bag and lo and behold had not been able to do so! It must indeed be very complicated for an airline that uses thousands of computers to figure out who the crew members on a specific flight where at a given date and then try and figure out how to contact them!

I knew as a matter of fact from some of my friends who worked at different airlines that all employees are on call 365/7/24 and accessible at all times. Hatay Pacific Hong Kong customer relations was not different or better than the Hatay Pacific customer "uncare" in New York, but they were starting a new play, using the same playbook. Delay, make it difficult, cause more frustration and suffering. Make the unhappy customer go away. Screw the customer! The gentlemen at Westminster City, London at Qwire Group would be proud.

Two days after my email, as if a magical wand had blessed the Hatay Pacific computers they had managed to contact the crew of the flight. The crew apparently rejected everything despite me providing the names and descriptions of the flight attendants that worked our part of the cabin. According to the crew our bag never existed! Fortunately we had our ticket's and boarding passes otherwise they might have said we never existed!

Just like Ravioli in the New York office, Lee having played the delay, cool off, wait for the opposing party to blink first and gain the moral high ground game; impressed on us that despite us trying to commit gross fraud they might compensate us if we presented receipts of the lost items. No mention of the damages due to the lost academic articles, publications and most important of all my doctoral dissertation proposal. Any College Professor or academic will know how much hard work is needed to put together a doctoral dissertation proposal. Hatay Pacific stole a year of my working life.

Despite everything I do show compassion to the crew, the 16 hour flight from Hong Kong to New York is very long and tiring. Mistakes may have been made. It's understandable. But the decent and ethical thing to do would be to own up to the mistake. Instead Hatay Pacific further escalated the matter by bringing in their expensive New York landmark building lawyers.

6: EXPENSIVE NEW YORK LAWYERS

Not only was Hatay Pacific not going to compensate us, they were ready to fight it out legally. I was given the name of their lawyer in New York.

Their address is at one of Manhattan's expensive landmark buildings:

Mr. John Doe
John Doe LLP
The Expensive Landmark Building
Expensive Manhattan Avenue
New York, New York

My apologies to Mr. John Doe at John Doe LLP, I have never met you, never done business with you and I am sure you are good people. But why would you want to work for the likes of small time criminals like Hatay Pacific Airlines? What happened to your oath of upholding "Justice" and practicing your profession "Ethically"?

The amount of compensation I am rightfully due as a result of Hatay Pacific losing my bag, damaging my health and taking away a year of work product is dwarfed by what Hatay would pay this expensive lawyer to write three or four memos and answer a few emails. Note the lack of an email address. You have to write and post a letter and send it by certified mail. Normal snail mail will not do as otherwise they would just pretend to never having received your letter and delay yet further.

High five! Bravo to Hatay Pacific! Doing everything to make it even more difficult and costly for the customer. I am but one individual facing a huge multibillion dollar organization. The most I can do is to take this to small claims court. The Hatay Pacific lawyers will do their best to carry this to a normal court where they will play the process of hiking up costs and legal expenses. You see where this is going? How can you prove negligence, willful negligence or wanton disregard when the 800 pound bully will stall, ask for extensions, launch appeals, play the change of venue process and any and all tricks in their book of dirty tricks?

Next I contacted the Better Business Bureau (BBB) of New York which lists arbitrating and solving such issues in its terms of reference. You guessed it, the BBB skimped out of doing its job by citing a technicality in my claim. The technicality could have been argued successfully both ways, but the BBB chose not to support the customer against a 800 pound Gorilla.

7: BATTLING HATAY PACIFIC ON SOCIAL MEDIA

What do you do after you tried everything to pursue your rights battling the unethical 800 pound gorilla for over a year? You name and shame them. Maybe public opinion would make the unethical and criminal organization reconsider its position? I opened a new front, the social media front, which I hoped would shame them.

Unfortunately the thing that I had not taken into account was that "shame" was not something Hatay Pacific had. Looking back I now see how naive I was. I had read several accounts of how unhappy passengers with horror stories took on airlines on social media; I remember the terminally ill war veteran that was denied service, the sick mother who wasn't allowed to fly back home from Europe because she was deemed too fat despite purchasing two seats etc..

Maybe using the social media would work with Hatay Pacific Airlines?

I started posting on their Facebook (FB) page and got back a swift standard reply that they would look into it. Nothing happened of course. It was just for show. So I posted again and again and again on all their FB pages. That's when the personal attacks started. Not from Hatay Pacific itself but from some seemingly "unaffiliated" but concerned citizens who seemed to support Hatay Pacific Airlines. Here are some of the funnier FB postings:

"Why was I posting on all the Hatay Pacific pages? How dare I?"

"My grammar was inadequate and my students as a result would learn little and fare badly in their lives".

"It was not "cool" for me to be posting like this"

Oh and the funniest part was, but I have to tell you the story first.

Soon after the sex scandals broke Hatay Pacific launched a very expensive advertisement campaign which aired on CNN, BBC and a host of other channels. The aim of the expensive advertisement campaign was to wipe out from consumers memory the slutty images of Hatay Pacific flight attendants as a result of the sex scandals and reposition and rebrand the Hatay Pacific air and ground crew (and the overall brand) as professional, responsive, efficient and caring.

Now let me ask you something and be true to yourself when you answer. Think of action movies and name ten male movie characters that all women in the movie will find irresistible and eventually either have sex with or want to have sex with. Well it's not her majesty's special agent "McKay, Jim McKay".

You guessed it, the Hatay Pacific business class advertisement closely emulates a classic special agent scene. The naughty special agent lookalike sits in Hatay Pacific business class when the flirting scene with the sexy flight attendant begins.

By the way, if you have watched this genre of movie you know that the special agent has a thing for flight attendants. I wonder what they were trying to do? What I perceived from the ad was "Fly Hatay Pacific business class and meet a Lily" !

You got to give it to them though. How best to leverage a sex scandal. The other ad Hatay Pacific launched was less glamorous. A more buxom looking Hatay Pacific ground attendant, albeit very helpful and very crafty approaches a distressed "Deer" or "Dear" in the headlights and steers them through the jungles of Hong Kong airport.

Lisa writes back to me stating that they might "consider" compensation with the right documentation and that I am free to take the matter to court. Back to square one. A friend living in Hong Kong came to the rescue and pointed out how sensitive Hatay Pacific is when it comes to the Hatay Pacific sex scandals. He even found and posted a number of the oral sex photos on the Hatay Pacific page. I so far had not had the inkling to take a look at them and saw them the first time when he posted them on the Hatay Pacific FB page. They were bad. There are also uncensored pictures which clearly show the Hatay Pacific captains organ being "processed" by the Hatay Pacific flight attendant. I am not going to post them here, but you can find them online when you Google "Hatay Pacific Sex Scandal".

The adventures of Lily in the cockpit! The adventures of Lily outside the cockpit! And apparently the adventures of Lily in five star hotels, the narrative and pictures available on FB page. The husband of a Hatay Pacific flight attendant's FB page wherein he pleads publically to Hatay Pacific executive management to put an end to the sexual exploits of his wife by Hatay Pacific captains and managers. I am not making any of this up, it's all available publicly.

You may have guessed that Hatay Pacific did not like me posting this explicit material on their FB pages and they had to change their FB modus operandi. As you may also have guessed I have been banned from their pages because they can't tolerate to get negative feedback and be shamed in front of their customers. You can no longer post discussions or pictures on their FB page. All customer input has to go through an approval process before it is posted. I think that this practice of censorship is widely used in undemocratic and autocratic countries and organizations. Wipe out the voice of dissent, eradicate all that is negative and rewrite history. Sounds like North Korea! I could of course get a new FB identity, use a different IP and computer and keep on posting. Today Hatay Pacific is spending more and more time to screen their social media activity. Additional man hours spent means additional costs. Hatay Pacific is losing money as a result.

Next, I took up the matter on the Linkedin social media platform.

Hatay Pacific utilized the same strategy as they had done on Facebook. They used "unaffiliated" group members to wear me down, or rather tried.

The comments were more vicious this time:

Comments that I don't deserve to fly Hatay Pacific, that I was a fraud, that it was entirely my fault and some even sharing Hatay Pacific internal process knowledge pertaining to what type of material Hatay Pacific uses on board and what kind of training Hatay Pacific stewardesses attend etc. (Well, they get some kind of training all right!). Then there were the lawyers who weighed in on my comments and pointed out the many loopholes that protected Hatay Pacific.

Many also weighed in on the Hatay Pacific price fixing scandal stating that many other airlines were involved in price fixing and alluded that this was "normal" and hence acceptable. The same approach was used to downplay the Hatay Pacific sex scandals. "All airlines have sex scandals, this one just became public". The Hatay Pacific sex scandal was thus deemed normal . Hey, if all of them do it, why should Hatay Pacific not do it. Gee, the others don't film the "Lisa" cockpit action and post it online. Have you never heard the saying, "You don't crap where you eat"?

Hatay Pacific finally had to step in when I trumped the "unaffiliated" lawyers by posting that it was the job of criminal defense attorneys to find loopholes in the law and legal processes to get their criminal employees out of jail so that they could go back to the robbing and murdering whoever it is that they rob and murder. This is exactly what they were trying to do, going through the Vienna and Warsaw conventions that dictated the rules of passage and how Hatay Pacific had the right to lose and destroy any private property and avoid any and all liability. False! Bunch of lies! Yet again!

According to the law there was gross negligence on part of Hatay Pacific if not outright willful negligence. Hatay Pacific commented that they were now ready to resolve the matter and that I should once again contact their customer service manager. I also posted what was to be my last post on the Hatay Pacific Linkedin group page (They locked me out!) and asked Hatay Pacific to donate whatever it is they owed me to a Catholic Church run Orphanage for drug addicted street children.

8: PLEASE DONATE

MY PLEA TO HATAY PACIFIC: PLEASE DONATE WHAT YOU OWE ME TO A CATHOLIC CHURCH RUN ORPHANAGE FOR DRUG ADDICTED STREET CHILDREN.

Every year I try to do the best that I can and to help in any way that I can and give something back to the community. Sometimes it is donations in cash or kind or pro bono work. There is so much poverty and need in the world and especially in the Philippines. Some of the neediest are drug addicted orphan street children that a Catholic Church run organization in Manila tries to help.

As naive as I am in believing in the good side of people and organizations, even I was shocked when Hatay Pacific changed the Linkedin forum posting rules and applied the same censorship as it had done previously with its Facebook page. My plea for a donation to a Catholic Church run orphanage for drug addicted street children fell on deaf ears. Think of how much good even a small donation of $10,000 could have done to feeding these children, helping them to recover and rehabilitate them. Think how normal they would have felt had they received Christmas gifts just like the millions of other children who would celebrate Christmas with their loving families in their warm homes.

Not a "peep". They could have even used this opportunity to promote themselves as a "caring" and "giving" organization. I even told them that there would be no need to mention my name. All my donations have been unanimous. Not a "peep" from Hatay Pacific.

This really infuriated me. How many billions of dollars did Hatay Pacific make last year? How much does the Hatay Pacific CEO make in a year? The amount of money that Hatay Pacific refused to donate for a good cause probably does not amount to even a millisecond of what they realize in revenues. Their mistake cost me a year of my work life and now a further two years fighting this unethical and criminal organization. This is the kind of organization that Hatay Pacific is.

9: CORPORATE SOCIAL RESPONSIBILITY

My contention so far has been that customer service at Hatay Pacific is designed and their employees trained so as not to serve customer needs but to ensure that the organization does not incur costs when it commits service delivery failures. Yes, for-profit companies have to pursue profits but should the organization not be ethically bound to correct its mistakes? Rather than invest in service delivery failure recovery procedures this organization tries to undertake all and any action to thwart the attempts of paying customers to ensure that Hatay at least meets the minimum legal threshold. I do not mention the minimum ethic threshold as there seems to be none at Hatay Pacific.

I have looked into the organization and organizational design of Hatay Pacific. I was surprised to see that the executive management in charge of operations were also sitting on the board of directors. Management science and empirical research has shown that organizations should ideally separate responsibility for short term operational performance from overall organizational accountability to stakeholders, if they want to limit agency cost and short term profiteering i.e. artificially increasing revenue by limiting competition in their home markets.

Most organizations have instituted corporate governance measures and corporate governance boards. Alas, my research revealed that Hatay Pacific has such a board and that is when I got all excited. Maybe the corporate governance board would do what is right? Closer inspection of the board revealed that the people who are operationally responsible for Hatay and who also sit on the board of directors are also exactly the same people that sit on the governance committee. Whereas corporate governance should ideally limit the number of hands in the cookie jar, in this case with this kind of organizational design It seems that the blind are paying lip-service to the deaf. What happens to good corporate governance when there is a lack of outside directors and auditors?

POST SCRIPTUM

What happens now?

Well I know what I am doing. I will keep on fighting Hatay Pacific to the end. I have done research on the internet and come across countless cases of Hatay Pacific causing damage to and threatening passengers. Now I don't know who those people were or what their grievance was or whether they were in the right or not, I can only comment on my case and my experience but there is a vast amount material out there about Hatay Pacific. Now, the rest is up to you. Please don't fly Hatay Pacific. Don't give them your business. That's the only thing that may hurt them. They don't care about anything else

Hatay Pacific now has a new slogan stressing the importance of human resources. Any organizational slogan related to how good their human resources are makes me think of engaged employees and capable managers who will go the extra mile to serve paying customers. The Hatay Pacific employees sure make Hatay Pacific a very special organization.

The Hatay Pacific managers and employees I have met so far were incompetent and unethical. My apologies to any good men and women employed by Hatay Pacific. Management necessitates action, problem solving, taking responsibility commensurate with authority and leadership. I can't see any of those traits in the Hatay Pacific employees I had to deal with. As a former executive I would be ashamed of working with the likes of these people.

I can already hear some of you. "McKay, you must be naive to expect anything else from such people, they are crooks". Some may say "It's the Chinese what do you expect". I assure you not. All the well seasoned executives in New York were Americans and all the senior management in Hong Kong are made up of British commonwealth expatriates.

Thank you for your time. I tried to share how 800 pound gorillas in the aviation industry operate. I hope none of this happens to you and please remember to never ever fly Hatay Pacific Airlines.

ABOUT THE AUTHOR

Jim Kayalar, DBA(ABD), MBA is a C level executive, management consultant, international author and Professor of business with over 30 years of business experience in 28 countries. Jim Kayalar's publications are distributed by Aspen House, Harvard Business Publishing, Ivey Publishing in North America and by CCMP France and ECCH England in Europe and by National Chengchi University in Taiwan. Jim Kayalar has led executive management training sessions and taught Executive MBA classes with focus on Entrepreneurship, Strategy, Marketing and Emerging Markets at prestigious business schools such as the University of London International Program, University of Bradford and University of Asia and the Pacific/IESE Business School Barcelona.

www.ingramcontent.com/pod-product-compliance
Lightning Source LLC
Chambersburg PA
CBHW070925180526
45168CB00005B/2159